EDGE CORE

Handbook

EDGE
Catholic Middle School Ministry

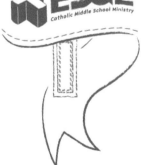

TOOLS TO ~~SURVIVE~~ THRIVE IN CATHOLIC MIDDLE SCHOOL MINISTRY

Quotes are taken from the English translation of the Catechism of the Catholic Church for the United States of America (indicated as CCC), 2nd ed. Copyright ©1997 by United States Catholic Conference – Libreria Editrice Vaticana.

The information contained herein is published and produced by Life Teen, Inc. The resources and practices are in full accordance with the Roman Catholic Church. The Life Teen® name and associated logos are trademarks registered with the United States Patent and Trademark Office. Use of the Life Teen® trademarks without prior permission is forbidden. Permission may be requested by contacting Life Teen, Inc. at 480-820-7001.

Our sincere thanks to all who contributed to this piece in its original form. A special thanks to Amanda Grubbs, Mark Hart, and Natalie Tansill.

Cover design by Casey Olson
Interior layout by Casey Olson

Copy editing by Natalie Tansill and Amanda Grubbs.

Published by Life Teen, Inc.
2222 S. Dobson Rd.
Suite 601
Mesa, AZ 85202
LifeTeen.com

Printed in the United States of America.
Printed on acid-free paper.

For more information about Life Teen or to order additional copies, go online to LifeTeen.com or call us at 1-800-809-3902.

TABLE of CONTENTS

STARTING STRONG

HELLO MY NAME IS:
EDGE

If you are reading this book that means that you have boldly and courageously said, "yes" to the call to work with middle school youth. Now you may be a pro at being a Core Member or you may be the newbie, but the reality is that no matter where you are in your ministry career, we all need a little refresher and revamp. So thank you for taking the time to read this Core Handbook. We hope that it blesses you in your ministry and provides you with the little boost that we all need from time to time.

We all need a little refresher and revamp.

It can all begin with one moment, a moment when you are sitting in the middle of an awkward small group and no one is talking. The youth are all picking at the carpet, their nails, their clothes, their hair, pretty much anything to keep them from making eye contact with you. Then, just when you think the silence might actually kill you, one of the youth in your small group whips a balloon out of absolutely nowhere and all of a sudden it's like your whole small group just ate a pound of pixie sticks. It is in these moments that you probably think to your self, "what the heck am I doing here?"

Well, my friend, welcome to the club. Everyone has had those moments when they wonder why they are in ministry, and why they have chosen to give their time to such a "crazy cause." It is essential that when you have these times of doubt you take the time to sit down, reflect, and pray about why you are a Core Member. When this happens you will either regain strength through a great conviction and passion for ministering to middle school youth or you will realize that it is time to move on and share your gifts in other ways. Both of which are *good* realizations because we have to go where Christ is calling us to serve.

WHAT IS EDGE?
The first step to really understanding *why* you are dedicated to something is to understand *what* it is that you are dedicated to. If you are reading this book, you probably know that Edge is a

middle school youth ministry program, and you are correct! But there is much more behind this movement than simply having another youth ministry program. Edge comes forth from the greater movement of Life Teen, which was originally established for high school ministry. As Life Teen began to grow, many parishes began asking how we could serve middle school youth in the same way as the high school teens. Thus Edge was created within the Life Teen movement and has been rapidly growing ever since.

The big picture behind the development of Edge has a few important components, which include:

• There are tremendous amounts of change for youth at this age both internally and in their social lives.
• Middle school youth begin to transition from the influence of their parents to the influence of friends and peers, and they need help and guidance.
• At this age, youth begin to question their identity.
• At this age, youth begin to question the purpose of their life.
• Middle School youth make decisions that can affect the rest of their lives.

Because there is so much changing in the lives of middle school youth, it is essential that they be introduced to the truth and love of Jesus Christ and the Church so that their lives can be transformed and led in a positive direction. Edge youth ministry strives to introduce the youth to the saving power and love of Christ in a few specific ways:

• Through fun and relevant catechesis.
• By connecting the youth to a loving community of friends.
• By having faithful adults present and who are committed to journeying with them.
• By reaching out in love and truth to lead youth closer to Christ.

WHAT IS A CORE TEAM?
As you begin to think more about what it is to be a Core Member you may be asking yourself some of these questions:

1. What exactly is *my* role in this?
2. What part do I have to play in the Edge program?
3. What exactly is a Core Team?
4. Am I really that important?

The aim of this book is to help you answer these and many more questions about being a Core Member. But to begin, keep in mind that:

- A Core Team contains many different people from many different walks of life.
- A Core Team comes together with a common mission to bring Christ to those they serve.
- There are many different qualities and duties of a Core Member, which will be discussed at length later in this book.
- The Core Team is an invaluable asset to your Edge program and your youth minister.

It would not be possible for a youth minister to successfully run an Edge Night without you. Imagine for a second an Edge meeting without any Core Members. There would be no one to greet the youth, the games would never work because one person cannot control that chaos, and the talks would not be heard by all the youth who are messing around when the youth minister is not looking. There also wouldn't be any small groups, and at the end of the night no one would be there to look out for all the youth as they leave. Undoubtedly, there would also be at least six wads of gum stuck in the carpet. While this is not even close to an exhaustive list of what would happen without Core Members, it at least shows you that this ministry would be a disaster without you!

You are an invaluable asset to your Edge program and your youth minister.

Have you ever heard the phrase "it takes a village"? Well it is true, it takes the combined efforts of many people to truly guide these youth to know Christ, and that is why we need you! A youth minister would be useless if it wasn't for the army of moms, dads, college students, single people, and high school teens backing them up and swatting down the paper airplanes. So as you recall all your horribly awkward encounters with middle school youth, remember you are here for a reason and you are needed.

WHY ARE YOU A CORE MEMBER?

There are countless ways that you could choose to spend your free time, yet here you are choosing to spend time with middle school youth every week. You have read about how important and essential a Core Team is to a youth minister, to running Edge

Nights, and to the youth they serve. Whether or not you are sure about your reasons for being on Core, spend time and ask Christ to lead you and guide you in this ministry by praying through the following questions:

1. Why are *you* on Core?
2. What is it that has drawn *you* to this point?
3. What is it that *you* feel called to bring to this ministry?

In order to be the best Core Member you can possibly be there has to be passion and drive behind your decision to join. Do not commit to these youth just because it is what you have done every year, or because some one forced you into doing it, or out of a need for attention. Serving on a Core Team is a calling from Christ and it must be done out of a conviction for doing His will.

Don't be afraid of this adventure you are embarking upon!

Christ needs committed workers in His vineyard. He needs people willing to be His hands and feet in the world. That being said, He does not abandon His workers, He is ever present with them. Do not be afraid of this adventure you are embarking upon! These youth need the best of you; they need the you that is ready to serve them selflessly as an example of Christ's love. So you must be prepared, you must be filled and fulfilled, for nobody can offer what they themselves do not have. So buckle up and open your hearts for what is to come.

SCRIPTURE SUGGESTIONS FOR PRAYER
Jeremiah 1:17
Jeremiah 29:11
John 15:15
John 13:15
Matthew 28:20
John 14:26
Philippians 4:13

ARE YOU READY TO BE WRECKED?

BY TRICIA TEMBREULL

Why do middle school youth around the globe return to parish halls and churches weekly for Edge? For some it is to grow in their faith. For others it's to hang out with their friends. For many more it is to develop a relationship with Christ. But on that first Edge Night, when the youth fearfully walk into a room full of people they do not know, it is the adult or high school Core Member who welcomes him or her with love and dignity that will keep him or her coming back week after week.

Speak truth when no one else will.

An Edge Core Member is so much more than someone who prepares the Gather, Proclaim, Break, and Send of each Edge Night. They also:

- Are invaluable witnesses to the youth and his or her parents that Jesus is real and a relationship with Him is not only possible but also fun.
- Remember more than the names of the people in their small group; they remember their interests, their struggles, their questions, and their doubts about God and His Church.
- Listen, pray, and love middle school youth as they are, yet at the same time challenge them to live fully as the man or woman God is calling them to be.
- Defend and protect the youth.
- Speak truth when no one else will.

Outside their ministry to the middle school youth, Edge Core Members:

- Hunger for a relationship with Christ.
- Are humble to admit that they do not know it all and will seek the answers through prayer, study, and the wisdom of Church leaders and fellow Core.

- Desire deeper relationships to help them on their faith journey, and they are willing to be vulnerable in sharing who they are with one another.
- Seek the Sacraments of the Catholic Church and point middle school youth to Christ and not to themselves.

Yet being a Core Member is still so much more than all of this. I remember when my two sisters joined Edge Core at their parish. Every week one of them would call me to me tell me about how God was speaking to their heart or how they learned something about the Church they never knew before. It was so exciting to hear the joy and wonder in their voices as they watched the middle school youth grow in their relationship with the Lord. It was even more beautiful to see how the youth's witness of faith challenged my sisters to live in a new way.

Whether you realize it or not, God is going to use this ministry and these youth to wreck your life. When you see the freedom of a middle school youth to worship without boundaries in adoration, your life will be changed. When you listen to stories that destroy the innocence of your middle school youth, your heart will break and you will partially understand the weight of sin that Christ bore on the cross. As you disciple these youth from middle school and beyond, you will see the glory of God revealed, and your heart will overflow with love.

God is going to use this ministry and these youth to wreck your life.

So much of this ministry as an Edge Core Member is intangible and you may never feel like you are making a difference, but your witness, your love, your prayer, and your example to the youth God has placed in your care will be an anchor in the midst of any storm that comes their way. Never doubt your effectiveness in ministry. Even when you do not hear it from your priests or Edge youth ministers, we are so thankful for your yes and cannot reach the middle school youth without you. Be aware that with Christ all things are possible (Philippians 4:13) even when your calendar, fears, and life are dictating another story. Keep your eyes centered on Christ and the Eucharist and everything you do for His glory will be magnified.

WHY I JOINED CORE TEAM

BY RYAN O'CONNELL

There are good reasons and bad reasons to join Core at your parish. Part of the discernment process involves making sure the good reasons are at the top, and the bad reasons are nowhere be found. If the reasons you want to join Core are to spend time with that other cute Core Member you have been checking out, or to get some free food, you are probably not called to this ministry. The same goes for wanting desperately to be admired by impressionable youth because your peers do not give you enough attention. Joining a Core Team is a serious call to serve, so you need to be serious about your reasons to join.

I have a responsibility to use my gifts for the glory of God.

When I was discerning whether I would join Core, I wrote out a list of my reasons. Here were my top five reasons for joining Core:

1. **I want to bring youth closer to Christ.**
   If I did not have a heart for youth, I could not serve in this ministry. Period. I feed off the energy of youth and love sharing truth with them. I want to lead them closer to Christ because I know they are the future of the Church. I know how much my faith has enriched my own life, thus I am compelled to share that with others, especially when they are young enough to avoid the unnecessary mistakes that often accompany young adulthood.

2. **I have a responsibility to use my gifts for the glory of God.**
   Since the call to evangelization applies to every baptized Christian, I know I need to develop a self-awareness of my gifts and talents, and pray about how I can best use them for the Kingdom. I realized that God has given me the ability to communicate my faith well and connect with youth. Thus, I realized that one of the best ways I could respond to that call to use my gifts and talents was by working with youth.

3. **Seeing youth draw closer to Christ brings me joy.**
For me, this ministry is fulfilling and joyful. It is also incredibly challenging, but the change I am blessed to witness in youth is reward enough. There is nothing like seeing a youth walk out of the confessional beaming and thanking you for encouraging them to go. Of course, all credit goes to God. But being used by the Spirit to change lives gives me an incalculable sense of purpose.

4. **I want to grow in my faith.**
It is nearly impossible to dive into ministry and not grow as a child of God. Youth have an incredibly accurate way of seeing right through you, and they can tell right away if there is a lack of sincerity or conviction in anything you share or teach. For me this is always a huge wake-up call to examine areas of my own faith. Being responsible for the formation of youth demands that I constantly pay attention to my own spiritual growth because I cannot share what I do not possess. I have to know what I am talking about, and believe what I'm talking about. It is somewhat startling to realize that if I give anything less than my best I might actually be harming their budding relationships with Christ.

5. **I need community.**
Serving on Core keeps me plugged into my parish and blesses me with meaningful, life-long friendships. My brothers and sisters on Core hold me accountable, challenge me, and support me when I am struggling. My Core Team is like family. While I am not best friends with all the Core Members, sharing in a common goal with so many different people helps me to grow in my own virtue and conviction of the ministry. Community is an amazing and irreplaceable benefit of ministry.

PART 1: TAKING IT FURTHER

1. What are your top five reasons for being a Core Member?

_____

_____

_____

_____

_____

_____

_____

_____

2. What is one specific skill or talent you have that you can
use in this ministry as a Core Member?

_____

_____

_____

_____

_____

_____

_____

3. What do you struggle with most when it comes to being a Core Member?

_____

_____

_____

_____

_____

_____

_____

_____

_____

_____

_____

_____

_____

_____

_____

FROM THE INSIDE OUT

BE A HEALTHY PERSON

Youth Ministry necessitates some really odd hours. Long after the Parish secretary has rolled the phones to voicemail, you are trying to track down 50 pens that actually write or 20 Bibles that never made their way back to the bookcase before your Edge kids arrive. By the time the last middle schooler is picked up, the last door gets locked and the last parking lot conversation ends, your last brain cell is probably running on overdrive. And even after all this, the adult Core still have laundry to do and high school Core Team Members still have homework to finish.

In order to get to the point where we become our strongest for God, we must begin where we are weakest.

The result? *Exhaustion*: mentally, socially, and emotionally. Youth ministry has left you spiritually uplifted but physically drained. It is at this point that unhealthiness can creep in. This is where we can quickly get disordered, spending so much time "taking care of" others – Edge teens, their families, and fellow Core Members – that we fail to take care of ourselves. This is also the dangerous time when we unconsciously begin to equate what we "do" for God (ministry) as being equal to spending time with God (prayer). As we start to see these things creeping up in our lives, it is important to take the time to stop and evaluate if you are really taking care of yourself.

This type of emotional, spiritual, and physical healthiness is something that we can all can do and should all strive for. In order to get to this point where we become our strongest for God, we must begin with where we are weakest. The enemy will not attack us where we are strong as readily as he will attack us where we are weak, lacking, or wounded. Identify those areas of your life in which the evil one goes after you.

- What are you most ashamed of or embarrassed about?
- What exterior or earthly things does the devil try to use to make you question your role on Core or your effectiveness with Edge kids?
- Are you self-conscious about your age, your weight, your

cultural "disconnect," or your lack of theological knowledge? Along with identifying where your weaknesses are it is important to have a game plan to help over come those weaknesses and to continue to grow. Consider the following questions to help you see areas in your life where you need to recommit and continue to improve.

- What things do you do to proactively stay healthy in mind, body, and soul?
- Do you have a daily prayer rhythm?
- What role does prayer play in your family's life and in your home?
- Do you stop to consider how your sleep schedule, work/school schedule, and diet affect your prayer life and ultimately, your relationship with God?
- What steps do you take to ensure that you are setting healthy boundaries for yourself?
- How do you protect and create time for just you and your heavenly Father?

The answers to these questions are directly proportional to how effective your ministry will be and how much fruit it bears both in your own life and in the lives of those young Edge souls entrusted to your leadership.

As you start to reflect on your own personal healthiness and different areas where you may need to improve, it is also important to remember that a huge part of living a healthy lifestyle also comes in how you are living out your vocation.

The beauty of a Core Team is that there are so many different people of different ages, backgrounds, and stages in their lives. Each person's life brings a unique perspective to ministry and enriches the whole community.

You will function best when you are living a healthy, balanced life.

As a human being you will function best when you are living a healthy, balanced life. This type of lifestyle has a lot to do with you physically, but there is also a huge aspect to living a healthy life that has to do with how you balance ministry and your vocation. In the pages that follow you will find different stories and different suggestions to continue to build a healthy lifestyle personally and as a married, single, or student Core Member.

SCRIPTURE SUGGESTIONS FOR PRAYER:
Psalm 103:2-5
1 Corinthians 6:19-20
3 John 1:2
Proverbs 3:5-8
Philippians 4:6-7

IT'S WORTH THE EFFORT

BY MARK HART

Having spent the past 20 years in full time youth ministry, I've failed in more ways than I could count. Those failures, however, have taught me more than I can express in just a few pages here about how to stay "healthy" when working in youth ministry...so please allow me to share seven practical suggestions with you.

Prayer must precede, imbue, and follow every "thing" you do each day.

Now, nothing I am about to suggest will be a revelation to you. It should not be. In hopes of increasing the *longevity in* and *joy* for ministry, however, I would like to throw out a few very simple truths that bear repeating for all of us if we want to be healthy.

1. *Keep Prayer Primary:* Prayer does not "help" your relationship with God. Prayer is your relationship. We have all heard the Martha and Mary comparison used to death, so how about this one, instead: Moses led over a million of God's children out of captivity (ministry), but in the end, it was his personal relationship and (more to the point) lack of trust in God that prevented him from entering into the Promised Land.

- Prayer must precede, imbue, and follow every "thing" you do each day.
- It's not enough to "do" things for God, we must just "be" with God.
- All we do must be in response to our daily relationship with God in prayer.

2. *Make Time to Exercise:* Ministry life can often feel like you are on a treadmill...so constantly "on the go" that you cannot slow down long enough to exercise. Sadly, though, most of us in ministry never make the time to actually jump on the treadmill. If that is how you feel – like there just "aren't enough hours in the day" – then you cannot afford *not* to exercise. It is an investment of time.

- Exercise will keep your heart healthy, increase your energy level, mental sharpness, daily efficiency, and self-confidence.
- Even getting out for a walk each day makes a significant difference. So get that heart rate up!
- Ironically, the harder you exercise the more energy you will have (in the long run) to build God's Kingdom here on earth.

3. *Receive Daily Bread:* Consider the words of Pope Emeritus Benedict XVI, **"What constitutes our faith is not primarily what we do but what we receive."** Essentially, he was telling us that "it's better to receive than to give" when Who we receive is, in fact, Jesus Christ. It is in our reception of the Lord's Sacramental grace(s) that we unleash our true Catholicism.

- Do everything in your power to make it to daily Mass.
- If that is absolutely impossible then – at the very least – schedule a Eucharistic encounter, daily, in adoration.
- We need the Eucharist, and we need it daily so don't put the spiritual main course for Catholics on the back burner

4. *'Fess up:* Don't walk...*run* to that confessional. However often you normally go, double or triple it. Since God looks at us from the inside out (1 Samuel 16:7), it is important to remember that sin is not spiritual cellulite, it is spiritual cancer. It needs to be dealt with and Christ loves us enough to give us His Sacraments and His priesthood to do just that.

- Love the Edge teens enough to care about your own sanctity.
- Try to get into a rhythm of monthly confession or even bi-monthly.
- Make the commitment to show up for every meeting in a state of grace.

5. *Drive Past the Drive-Thru:* You know the dilemma: you are hungry but you did not pack any food. You have twenty minutes before Core Members begin arriving for an Edge Night. So you run out for some fast food before the meeting or even worse you hit the drive-thru on your way home. The problem is that the "food" (yes, I use quotes) has a long lasting and detrimental effect on our energy level, metabolism, and waistline. In cases like these, taste makes waist. (Don't you love stupid word play? I do.) The reason so many Core Members and Youth Ministers feel like garbage is because they eat it.

- Make the time to eat well.
- Take the time to pack lunches or dinners.
- Keep healthy snacks within reach.

Here are a few sobering stats for all of us:

- A *McDonald's* Quarter Pounder with Cheese and medium fries contains 890 calories and 45 grams of fat; throwing in a medium Coke adds an additional 58 grams of sugar.
- If your conscience tells you that *Starbucks* is far healthier, think again. A blueberry scone has 460 calories, 22 grams of fat and 61 grams of sugar. Oh, and that Venti coffee with cream? It'll come in at about 315 calories and 14 grams of fat.

> Do everything you can to make your Sabbath time sacred and model for others how to do the same.

6. *Get some Sabbath (Rest):* Keeping holy the Sabbath is easier said than done when Sundays might be the day your program meets. If your ministry schedule necessitates that your "Sabbath" be a Monday or a Friday, for instance, it ought to be spent predominantly in prayer, rest, and fellowship with God and family/neighbor. If it is not, it is time to radically redefine your schedule and approach. Spend some time in honest prayer about your week.

- Have chores, tasks, and commitments taken the place of Sabbath rest?
- Is it time to simplify?
- Has "honoring the Sabbath" been reduced to making it to Mass on time?

Sabbath rest is about far more than one hour at Mass. It is about freeing yourself from everything else.

> Laughter ought to be a rule for living.

- Eliminate screens.
- Refuse to use social media.
- Read a book...read His Book.
- Have conversations with God and with His children. Eat with your family or friends.

- Do everything you can to make your Sabbath time sacred and model for others how to do the same.

7. *Laugh More:* Laughter is not a suggestion. It is not a "goal." Laughter is one of God's greatest gifts to us. Unholy laughter is a rejection of truth, but holy laughter is a joyful rejection of cultural mistruths and it keeps you young in mind and heart. Laughter ought to be a rule for living. God laughs (Psalm 2:4). So ask yourself:

- What activities bring me the holiest joy?
- Which relationships bring me the holiest joy?
- What movies or television shows make you laugh the most?
- Figure out what makes you laugh and then put in on your weekly calendar.

MARRIAGE AND MINISTRY

BY CHRIS BENZINGER & MARK HART

Balance is a good thing; everyone loves and desires balance. I like to watch the incredible balancing acts at circuses, and as a general rule, I like not falling over when I stand on one foot. But what I like more than all these things is balance in my life, especially when it comes to figuring out the perfect balance between marriage, family, and ministry.

When we try to figure out how to make everything "work" in our lives, or when we are struggling with balance between our marriage and ministry, we must first go to the Lord. God loves you, God loves your spouse, and God loves your ministry. That being said, we must reevaluate how we go about finding balance in our lives. We need to start shifting our focus to what is at the center of our lives, rather than just focusing on all of the things that we are trying to balance because:

God loves you, God loves your spouse, and God loves your ministry.

- If balance is our ultimate goal, then something in our lives always wins and something always loses.
- The two things we love (marriage and ministry) will seem opposing to one another and pull against one another, and at any moment we have to choose between the two.
- Our efforts will become exhausting and we will get burnt out.

Surprisingly, burn out is not because we do too much but rather because our lives are disordered. If living an ordered life becomes a new goal rather than finding "balance," then:

- We will no longer have to choose one thing over another.
- Our vocation and our ministry will be a fruit of the order in our lives.

- Our lives will no longer be focused on finding the perfect percentage of time to a lot to different activities, but rather on learning to live an ordered, fruitful life.

As you shift your focus from a balancing circus act to living an ordered life, a good image to keep in mind is that of the tree from Psalm 1. This tree is "planted near streams of water, that yields its fruit in season; its leaves neither wither; what ever they do prospers" (Psalm 1:3). The reason why this tree always prospers is because its roots sink deep into this living water, which is the Lord. The reason why the tree yields fruit is because God is at the core and He is the source of its life.

If we want our marriage to thrive and our ministry to be fruitful, we must dig the roots of our tree—the roots of our lives—into the love of the Lord. This is not something that is new, and we all know that we need a personal relationship with the Lord. But nonetheless, it is only when this relationship is at the center of everything, when the Lord is at the root of our lives, that order will come about and we will bear fruit that never withers.

There are always sacrifices and blessings when you are married and working in ministry. Marriage is clearly primary, and when balance is no longer the goal but rather striving to center your life on God, then your vocation will become a blessing to your ministry. The two will no longer be opposing because your ministry will flow out of your vocation and your fruitfulness will no longer be dependent on how good you are at your balancing act, but rather on the strength and love of Christ.

Start very simple, stick to something, celebrate your success and keep diving deeper as you spiritually grow.

That being said here are a few practical things to keep in mind on how to help renew and sustain a healthy marriage while being involved in ministry:

1. *Establish a rhythm of prayer.* You must have a rhythm of prayer in your own life, with your spouse, and with your family. Creating a rhythm of prayer is not just another thing to add to your list, but rather it is a change of perspective. Start very simple, stick to something, celebrate your success and keep diving deeper as you spiritually grow.

If your spouse does not pray:

- Ask him or her what is going well in life and what is hard in life.
- Share your hearts with each other.
- Through all of this help your spouse to start recognizing God in daily life.

If you have kids, remember prayer will be continually changing:

- Keep in consideration their age in what you expect from them.
- Teach them simple Catholic prayers and stick with one until they have it memorized.
- Help them learn to be thankful for things, and to pray for themselves and others.
- Do not be afraid to try new things.

2. *Support your spouse.* Sacrifices have to be made when it comes to ministry and marriage. We must redefine what "support" means. Support does not mean, "do whatever you want and I won't say a word about it." Support comes from the Latin word *supportare,* and that literally means, "to carry from below."

If only one of the two people minister on the Core Team:

- Support must come from both people, and special attention needs to be paid to the spouse not on Core Team.
- The spouse who is not on Core Team can support the other by staying home and managing the house during Edge Nights.
- The spouse on Core Team *must* prayerfully and thoughtfully seek ways to support the marriage and household before he or she leaves to serve the youth.

If you do ministry together:

- Don't let ministry become the only thing you do together.
- Set up boundaries and times you will not talk about ministry.
- Have friends outside of the Core Team.

3. *Communication* is key. Once you've entered into the Sacrament of Holy Matrimony, God now loves you most directly through your spouse and you are called to offer the love of Christ, first and foremost, to your spouse. Those working in ministry can never allow those who are not to feel second or third on the list of priorities. That is not living out the Sacrament. To avoid this requires:

- Your presence, both physical and emotional.
- That you allow your brain to step off the hamster wheel of ministry at home.
- You to be truly be present to your husband or wife and family by keeping your primary vocation, primary.

The Sacrament is stronger than you are.

4. *Create a family mission.* A family mission reveals what is most important to you, your spouse, and your family. Write those things down and do what is necessary for your family to represent your mission together. This is something you can refer back to often and especially when you feel like you are getting off track. To start making your own family mission, here are a few questions to consider:

- What are you going to commit to as a family?
- What do you want your family to look like?
- What are your goals?
- What is at the center of your family?

You can do it. You can have a healthy, vibrant marriage and also a healthy, balanced ministry life. It is difficult. It takes incredible work. It takes unbelievable thought and great humility. It takes constant communication. But it does work. It can work. And when you feel too weak to make it work anymore, remember, the Sacrament is stronger than you are.

BEING SINGLE IN MINISTRY

BY RYAN MILLER

At some point between the speed of my metabolism as a 15-year-old and the strands of grey hair I've noticed as a 28-year-old, I, like most single people, have struggled with staying healthy. Getting older is sometimes fun, but with it come challenges of physical and emotional health, balances between work and relationships, and the changing spiritual dynamic of life.

I will confess, I have not always been the healthiest person and I am prone to the late night Taco Bell runs. However, with the challenges I have faced come some insight that might make your life better as a single person while working with middle school youth.

So, why is being healthy really important to ministry? The primary reason is theological: we are both soul and body. And so many of us let go of ourselves to focus on the people we minister to. So here are a few quick tips for on staying healthy as a single person in ministry:

1. **Emotional and Mental Health**
   We all have wounds from our past. Sometimes being single can be a great blessing to give us time to heal from those wounds. Being an emotionally balanced person is obviously important when ministering to young people. Here are some things you can do to help you in this area.

- Ask for help from a counselor if necessary.
- Develop habits that make you a more emotionally and mentally balanced person.
- Integrate your faith with your emotional well-being. You will begin to develop a deeper understanding of God's love and learn to trust His plan for your life with greater freedom.

2. **Friendships and Community**
   Being on Edge Core, you will no doubt develop friendships with other Core Members. But Core is not the first place you should

seek out friendships. Here are some tips for building a healthy community:

- Have good, healthy friends outside of Core.
- You can and should spend time with Core Members outside of Edge Nights.
- Your primary focus for your involvement with Edge should be to serve the youth not to make new friends.

3. **Work and Ministry**
The primary reason most people do not join Core is because they are "too busy" and usually this means you are working too much outside of your work day or stressed at your job.

- If your life is dominated by stress, then it may be time to take a critical look at what role work has in your life.
- As someone who has given too much of his time and effort into work, I can tell you that your identity can quickly shift from being a son or daughter of God to being a un-joyful worker.
- Ministry requires not just your time, but also your emotional presence and a deeper spiritual life, it is important to prayerfully discern how much extra time you spend working.

4. **Family**
So you are single. You may have just moved into an apartment, started a new job, maybe in a new city, and you want to be on Core. Great! And then your mom and dad want you to come back home on a Sunday night for dinner. What do you do when family life and time on Core conflict?

- Family life can be tricky when you are single, and you have to figure out the balance that works best for you.
- It is essential to maintain good relationships with your family because this helps you minister well.
- Middle school youth need good examples of people who love their families.
- If you have a family that is not so great, it is important that you have a healthy outlook on family life so that you can relate to and help those youth who are struggling with the same thing.

5. **Vocation**
Single and ready to mingle? Hard to find a good Catholic mate? You might think Core would be a perfect place to start finding someone to marry, and while this could be a possibility, joining Core for this reason alone is a recipe for disaster.

- The dynamics of a Core Team can be greatly affected by the drama of relationships, so it is important that you prayerfully discern any sort of relationship with another Core Member.
- Finding a spouse should not be the goal of your time on Core Team.
- Holiness, friendship, and a common mission of serving should help direct your relationships with other Core Members.

6. **Spiritual Health**
   Your singleness offers you an incredible opportunity to develop a deeper relationship with God. As a single person, you also have a lot of opportunities to ignore your relationship with God. Your choices now can dramatically help or hinder your ability to be an effective Core Member. There are a few important things that can help you grow in your spirituality:

Your singleness offers you an incredible opportunity to develop a deeper relationship with God.

- Commit to personal prayer, frequenting the Sacraments, and spiritual reading.
- Spiritual direction, and personal retreats are also at your disposal to help you develop into a spiritually healthy person.
- Do not identify your time on Core as your personal prayer time.
- Do not neglect your own soul.

We are all asked to serve God in this life, but our true identity as sons and daughters is bigger and more important than any work that we do for Him. As single people, we can often get wrapped up in doing things. It makes us feel good. We know we're helping out and we feel like we belong. But our true identity is the most important part of our lives. Middle school youth are developing their identities. They need to see you live out your true identity so that they can find their own sense of worth it as a son or daughter of God.

YOU ARE A STUDENT, SO BE A STUDENT

BY AMY BRANT

When I was in high school I loved being on Edge Core. It was such a blessing for me to be able to listen to the middle school youth, journey with them week after week, and watch them grow in all the ways that God was calling them. I found their lives to be living testaments and sources for a renewal of my own faith. They challenged me to go deeper in my own personal prayer life and to participate more fully in Life Nights. My absolute favorite part of the week was the time I was able to spend at Edge with the youth. However, I found that the only way to be a good Core Member was to be fully attentive to the middle school youth, and I quickly found that that meant not saving my homework until right before or after Edge. Yes, I was called to be an Edge Core Member. Yes, I loved it. But ministry is never an excuse to not be obedient to the state of life you're in, and mine was that of being a student.

By being a student, you are actually loving God and honoring Him.

But what does school have to with this anyway?

Well, as teenagers in high school or young adults in college, you are called to the life of a student. It is something that God has asked of you. We are called to love God with all our mind, heart, soul, and strength and that includes doing your best at what He has asked of you. So, by being a student, you are actually loving God and honoring Him.

As a Core Member, you want to let God in and push yourself out. You want Him to increase and for you to decrease so that you can be open to letting Him work through you and speak through you for the good of the middle school youth. In order for this to happen:

- You need to have a clear mind and a pure heart ready for each Edge Night.
- You cannot be thinking about all your homework and tests coming up.
- You need to learn to balance your time wisely.
- Have homework completed and completed well before Edge Night so you can have a clear mind and really focus on the youth you are serving.

If you take the time and effort to become a good student, you will find being a good Core Member will easily follow.

If homework is extremely burdensome to you and you find it easy to procrastinate (I do, too), then offer up your study time for one of the youth in your small group and then do all of your homework without complaining. I'm sure it will bear a lot of fruit in your life as well as in theirs.

What are some practical ways to manage some of these things you need to do so that you can be a better student and be more present to the middle school youth?

1. **Social Media.** Turn off social media while you are studying. I know it is tough, but let's be real:

- There is no picture on Instagram that is going to help you with those Geometry proofs.
- There is no app on Facebook to balance a chemistry equation for you.
- There is certainly no 140 character tweet that can finish your English paper.

2. **Discipline.** I always had the mantra of "Due Tuesday? DO Tuesday!" but that lacked prudence. It was exhausting to complete an entire homework assignment, which I was given a week to complete, in one evening (or the morning before class). Here is a tip I learned the hard way:

- Do a little every day. If you divide out your work over several days, you will find homework less exhausting to complete if you are prudent and diligent.

3. **Have a routine.** This will not only help you be a better student, but also a better child of God. Here are some tips:

- Have 15-30 minute windows that you dedicate each day to prayer and study.
- Maybe you wake up 15 minutes before you need to wake up and dedicate that time, every morning, to reading and reflecting on Scripture.
- Maybe you put off your after-school snack for thirty minutes and dedicate your first chunk of time after you get home to studying.
- Keep these windows in place; you will have more free time to do other things and less stress when big assignments come up.

I know it can be tough to balance ministry and homework. However, it is an important feat to make. No matter how hard it may seem, you can do it. And if you take the time and effort to become a good student, you will find being a good Core Member will easily follow.

PART 2: TAKING IT FURTHER

1. What is one thing you can commit to changing in your life to become a healthier person?

_____

_____

_____

_____

_____

2. What is one thing you can commit to in order to become a holier person?

_____

_____

_____

_____

3. According to your vocation, what is one tip or suggestion you can take and apply to your life?

_____

_____

_____

_____

_____

4. What makes you laugh? How can you make it a part of your everyday life?

_____

_____

_____

_____

_____

_____

_____

_____

_____

_____

_____

BUT WHY ARE THEY SO CRAZY!?

MEET YOUR MIDDLE SCHOOLERS

Imagine your parish meeting hall. Picture the sterile walls covered with felt banners of Catholic "artwork." Take in the hollow echo of every whisper bouncing off the linoleum floor. Bask in the aroma of fire-hazard coffee makers left on too long while the residue at the bottom of the pot fuses itself to the glass. Notice every fake plant, every carpet square and each picture of every former Pastor. The room is empty, quiet and seemingly large.

Middle school is such a beautiful celebration of insanity.

Now...imagine it filled with middle school students.

It is amazing how quickly the serene and almost "dead" scene shatters to one overflowing with life and awkwardness, isn't it?

Middle school is such a beautiful celebration of insanity. The hyperactivity and hormones meet in an adolescent blender of puberty that can leave even the most patient soul overwhelmed by the noise and relative goofiness. That goofiness, however, is only skin deep. Under every gangly or pint-sized young Edger's maturing exterior lay a pure soul seeking attention, hoping for affirmation, and wanting acknowledgment that they not only "exist" but deeply matter.

Many of the Edge youth before you will be straining to seem comfortable in situations where they are clearly not. You can notice so much about certain youth when you pay attention to their habits.

- Watch them move around the parish hall in packs and herds.
- Pay attention to how they seek the opinion of "pack leaders" or validation from one another.
- Notice how they do and do not interact with the opposite gender.
- Notice how the most basic human exchanges vary, mature, and become increasingly emotional in the three short years between 6th and 8th grade.

As you begin to interact with these youth you have observed, you will probably encounter that your conversations will vastly vary from youth to youth.

- Some from this screen-based generation will want to begin conversations with you but not know how.
- Others will speak merely to fill the uncomfortable silence. Still others will talk about seemingly non-sensical topics that matter a great deal to them but that you are not well versed in.
- Some will avoid eye contact because it makes them uncomfortable and others because they have been conditioned to do so at home or school.

You will interact with Edge youth who are pure as the snow, fiercely protected by their parents in an epic battle to shield them from the obvious darkness of modern culture. You will also share prayer and conversation with middle school youth who have encountered far more than their young minds and hearts were ever designed to withstand. There are many sin-tattered young souls who are in need of God's mercy and the promise that a broken home or past does not mean a hopeless future. The challenging reality as a Core Member is that you may encounter the broad spectrum of these different life stories in the very same small group at any given Edge Meeting!

So at the end of the day, it matters little if you like video games or anime or the latest music sensation. You won't laugh at the same jokes and many of those you do laugh at will be in a sincere attempt to protect their dignity rather than a salute to the comic gods...and that is more than okay. Your validation is not inauthentic, it is beautiful and necessary and appreciated. Edge youth need to know that their presence is noticed and that they matter.

SCRIPTURE SUGGESTIONS FOR PRAYER:
Matthew 11:28-30
Luke 15:7
John 13:34
Romans 8:28
1 Timothy 4:12

ADOLESCENT DEVELOPMENT

BY CHEYENNE D. VASQUEZ,
MARRIAGE AND FAMILY THERAPIST INTERN LIC. #73778

Middle School youth are at a time in their life when they are undergoing tremendous developmental changes. Therefore we must keep in mind all the transitions they are going through and realize that no two youth will act or react in the same way to the same things, we cannot expect them to be a "one size fits all." As you continue to figure out how best to cater to their constant craziness, take into consideration all the different areas that are changing for them. Let's take a look at the five major ways that middle school youth will undergo change and the effect it has on their lives:

> We cannot expect them to be a "one size fits all."

1. **Physical Changes:** Middle school adolescents are experiencing drastic hormonal changes. They begin to struggle with:

- Their self-image can create anxiety and curiosity in their everyday life.
- They can become victims of society's image of beauty.
- They are approaching (or have approached) puberty and have begun to understand and desire to experiment with human anatomy.

For the young women specifically:

- They are beginning menses.
- They have altered their mood from time to time.
- Their bodies also begin to change preparing themselves for motherhood and receiving the attributes they need in order to procreate.

For the young men:

- Their smell, voice, and body changes.
- These changes can play into how they view their own self-image, making their physical appearance more important.
- Their energy level can be heightened due to hormonal changes.

Tips for Core Team:
- Be good role models for modesty in the way you dress, especially women for the young ladies.
- Do not ever make any negative comment about a youth and their appearance, no matter how awkward they may be, rather always be uplifting and affirming.
- When you split up into girls and guys sessions, or girls and guys small groups help them work through some of the issues they may be struggling with this area (remember you always must be in compliance with Safe Environment rules).

2. **Psychological Changes:** Imagine walking around all day with a massive zit on your face and everyone is staring at you: this can pretty much sum up the life of most youth. They are completely self-conscious of what others think about them, and at this stage in their lives, they are willing to compromise in order to be accepted. Often times at this age middle school youth are struggling with:

- Finding their "place," which means that they are trying to find the right clique to hang out with at lunchtime.
- The stress of constant change.
- Being emotionally sensitive, needing to find good community and positive relationships.
- Search for an identity.
- Dealing with the loss of childhood and are transitioning into adulthood. Usually, females are more willing to verbally share emotions than males.

> Middle school youth are struggling with finding their "place."

Tips for Core Team:
- Be welcoming to every youth that comes to Edge and help create an environment of a loving community.
- Get to know the names of the youth and encourage them to get to know each other better. Also help them to develop new friendships.

- In small groups, appropriately model how to share emotions and be compassionate towards the youth as you guide and affirm them.

3. **Cognitive Changes:** Cognition is the way individuals intake and process information. Sometimes you can see middle school students soaking up moral theology of the Church because the light bulbs in their heads are finally going on. Just as the middle school youth are growing physically, they are also changing intellectually.

- During puberty, youth move from a concrete way of thinking to an abstract way of thinking.
- Their previous idea of thinking of the world as only happy and sad makes way for abstract thoughts.
- Deeper moral thinking and decisions are also heightened during this time.
- Middle school youth are not concerned with the future but rather the present, and tend to fail at thinking prior about consequences to their actions.

Tips for Core Team
- Challenge the youth in their thinking and processing skills, but also be patient and understand that they are at all different levels of intellectual development.
- Help the youth to process through their decisions and help them to begin to piece together the connection between actions and consequences.
- Do not talk too much in small groups; rather give them an opportunity to begin to express their feelings and ideas of different topics, and nurture their growing intellect.

4. **Relational Changes:** During the middle school years, there is a marked shift in a youth's life from primary relationships with family and parents to primary relationships with friends. The child who would not leave mom or dad's side is now thoroughly embarrassed to be seen with his or her parents in public. Prior to middle school, children depend greatly on their parents for love, support, affirmation, and guidance, etc. As they enter middle school, these same children now begin:

Just as the middle school youth are growing physically, they are also changing intellectually.

- Seeking love, support, and affirmation and guidance from their friends and peers.
- To recognize that their parent(s) is/are not perfect, have problems, and this can create relational problems between them and their parent(s).
- To make decisions they know are wrong in their quest to conform and not stand out among their peers.
- To do whatever it takes to keep their friends and make new ones so that they will not be alienated or lonely.

Tips for Core Team
- Always reinforce the importance of family and parents, make a point to meet the parents of the youth and help them to feel more involved in the ministry and the life of their child.
- Create a positive environment for the youth to make new friends and model to them as a Core Team what good friendships and community look like.
- Address their struggles with loneliness and reinforce the fact for them that Christ is always present and they are never truly alone.

5. **Spiritual Changes:** The cognitive development of middle school youth is one of the major influences in their spiritual development. As previously discussed, youth move from concrete thinking to abstract thinking during their cognitive development. This has a huge role in their spiritual development as they start to:

- Think about and process the deeper meanings within Scripture, teachings of the Catholic Church, and their personal relationship with Jesus.
- Transition from the faith of their parents to their own faith.
- Deal with doubts and questions about the faith.

Tips for Core Team
- Do not be afraid to help the youth go deeper in their spirituality and relationship with Christ and be present with them in their doubts and questions.
- Be patient as you guide them through the teachings of the Church and address their doubts with truth and love.
- Teach them how to find the answers to their questions on their own and help instill in them the ability to use Scripture and the Catechism to grow in their faith.

PART 3 : TAKING IT FURTHER

1. What intimidates you the most about working with middle school youth?

_____

_____

_____

_____

_____

_____

_____

_____

2. What do you love most about working with middle school youth?

_____

_____

_____

_____

_____

_____

_____

_____

3. What is one thing you learned about adolescent development that will help you minister better to the youth?

_____

_____

_____

_____

_____

_____

_____

_____

_____

_____

_____

_____

_____

_____

_____

_____

4

THE CORE OF CORE

BEFORE THE EDGE NIGHTS

You have had an opportunity to sit and reflect on your decision to be a Core Member. You have continued the ongoing process of bringing your life into balance. You have been given a boost in your spirituality and vocation. Now it's time to get into the core of what a Core Team is all about. While it does vary from youth group to youth group how a Core Team is run, there are some basic things that every Core Member should be prepared to do.

HELP THE YOUTH MINISTER

Get into the core of what a Core Team is all about.

Every Core Member is called to be a valuable asset to the youth minister. To answer the call to be on a Core Team is to answer the call to obedience. You are there for many reasons, but one of the main ones is to do the things the youth minister could not do! It is essential that you keep a few things in mind when assisting your youth minister.

- Bring it! Bring your "A" game. Come with a good attitude ready to participate, serve, and bring Christ to others.
- You are a part of a team and that requires sacrifice. To serve as a Core Member means to put another's welfare ahead of yours.
- You opinion is valuable, but ultimately you are called to be obedient to your youth minister, your pastor, and the teachings of the Catholic Church.

RELATIONAL MINISTRY

Another huge aspect of being a Core Member is relational ministry. Relational ministry is simply being present to the youth at the Edge Night and outside the Edge Night. It is all about being a positive support for them as they journey through the hardships of life. As you know, you are here not only to serve your youth minister but also to be a positive witness and guide for the youth that you serve. So much of what you do is not about the tasks you perform, or the talks that you give, but about who you are and how you show the youth that you care about them. Here are a few things to keep in mind:

- Be yourself!
- Simply love the youth.
- Be a positive witness to youth at all times.
- Listen to them and speak truth into their struggles.
- Practice what you preach.
- Be present at various events (Edge Nights, Bible studies, sports games, plays, concerts, graduation parties, musicals, etc.).
- Follow your Safe Environment guidelines.

The whole reason to do relational ministry is because the youth will not care about what you have to say until you show them that you care about them. Once they know they can trust you, then they will be willing to follow you towards Christ.

It is necessary for your efforts as a Core Team to be rooted in a relationship with Christ.

There are many ways to do relational ministry. But the core of it is that you just simply love the youth and witness to them the love of Christ. As you participate in each part of the Edge Night keep in mind this call to relational ministry. Be present in every game, in every activity, in every small group. There is never a time that relational ministry stops, it is just a part of being on Core Team and ministering to youth.

PRAY AS A CORE TEAM

The importance of prayer as a Core Team cannot be emphasized enough! It is essential not only for your own well being but also for your ministry to be fruitful. Just like it is necessary for the roots of your life to be grounded in a relationship with Christ, it is necessary for your efforts as a Core Team to be rooted in a relationship with Christ. Your faith and conviction will be challenged by these youth, so you need as much prayer as you can get! Also having a solid prayer time together as a Core Team helps to build your community.

ENVIRONMENT

When we are able to transform a simple gym or classroom into a game show set, a jungle safari, or a comfortable home living room, we can change a youth's whole outlook on Edge. The intentionality behind the Environment of an Edge Night is to make it something special, something different each week to keep things exciting and new. This may not be your favorite part of doing ministry, but the way that the room is set up and decorated can have an enormous impact on the youth's mentality during the whole Edge Night.

- Arrive early to help set up the Edge Night and stick around to help clean up.
- Help gather props.
- Use your creativity!

AT THE EDGE NIGHTS

Along with being the best asset to the youth minister and making relational ministry your second nature, there is also the concrete task of helping Edge Nights run smoothly. There is something for the Core Team to do in every step of the night even if it is not obvious at first, don't worry you are essential at all times even if you are not the one running the night!

GATHER

This portion of the night covers the span of time from when the youth walk through the doors up until the main teaching is being given. This time is intended to help the youth get comfortable with being at Edge and also to prepare them for the rest of the night. While this may not seem like the most important part of the night, it is in fact one of the greatest times for you to grow in relationship with the youth, to learn their names, to talk with them, and to have fun!

Every youth should be acknowledged when they come through the doors.

WELCOME

Welcoming the youth who come to Edge is a huge role of the Core Team. There is no way one person can greet every youth, but between the youth minister and the entire Core Team, every youth should be acknowledged when they come through the doors.

- Greet every youth you see as they come in.
- Pick a handful of youth to know by name and greet them specifically at every Edge Night.
- Just talk to them, even though it can be really awkward.

When starting conversations with middle school youth, try to avoid asking questions that can be answered with one word. Here are a few helpful conversation starters if you're ever at a loss.

- Hey how are you? What is your name? What grade are you in?
- What do you like to do for fun?
- What was the best part of your weekend (or day)?

GAMES

When playing games during the Gather activities, it makes a huge difference for them to see adults willing to be silly and crazy with them. So do not be afraid to jump in and have fun!

• Don't just run the games, but participate.
• Be present and play even if you are not good at the game.
• Do not get overly competitive or play just to win; help the youth to feel comfortable and to have fun.

SKITS

There are many different types of skits that can be done, but whether it is a funny two minute skit or a serious ten minute drama, they all should be planned out properly and rehearsed. There should be no "winging it" when it comes to skits, so make sure to participate to the fullest and be prepared for them.

• Memorize your lines and practice the skit beforehand.
• Don't turn your back on the crowd and speak loudly and clearly.
• For funny skits, always be appropriate and keep it clean.
• In dramas, make sure that it is clear that Christ is always the hero.
• Be yourself, over exaggerate, and make it your own!

PROCLAIM

Be silly and crazy with them.

The Proclaim section of the night is generally the time during the Edge Night when the youth minister or Core Member gives the main teaching. This can be one of the trickiest sections of the night because this section contains the most important information for the faith formation of the youth. Because most middle school youth have the attention span of a gold fish it is important to make your time count when it comes to the Proclaim. Also if you are not the one giving the talk, make sure to sit among the youth and be an example of attentive listening, and if necessary break up youth who are talking or correct those who are misbehaving and not paying attention.

GIVING A TALK

The "talk" or "proclamation" is when the topic for the night is covered. It is one of the most important parts of the night because it is here that the youth are introduced to a new aspect of Christ and the teachings of the Church. As a Core Member, it is important to play to your strengths.

- Practice your talk beforehand. Pray about it and have a clear point. Always keep Christ at the center of everything you teach.
- Keep it quick. Most youth don't pay attention for more than 10 minutes.
- Make it relevant; the youth should be able to tell you what your talk was about and how it applies to their lives.

As a Core Member, it is important to play to your strengths.

GIVING A WITNESS

There may be a time when a personal testimony is needed to drive home a point or a teaching. This is different from the talk or proclamation because you are speaking from personal experience rather than explaining a Church teaching. A time when you can tell the youth, "Hey I went through this and then Christ transformed my life and look at where I am now." You don't have to tell your entire life story. Make your testimony relevant, clear, concise, and give God the glory.

Here is a brief guideline on how to give a good testimony:

- Explain what your life was like before you came into a relationship with Christ or before you really understood and appreciated being Catholic. Make sure not to glorify sin.
- Explain what Christ did to break into your life in a new way, how He transformed you and what changed in your life because of it.
- Talk about how your life changed after this encounter with Christ or the Church. How did you respond to a call from Christ? How is your life better now? Make sure to always point to Christ's victory in your life especially over sin.

BREAK

All hands on deck for this portion of the Edge Night! This is the time when the youth really get to delve into what they just learned from the talk and process how it really applies to their lives. The main way that this is done is in small groups.

SMALL GROUPS

Usually a small group consists of one to two Core Members and anywhere from five to ten youth per group. For middle school youth too it is suggested that they remain with the same small groups all year so that they can grow in trust and community with one another. While this may be one of the most challenging parts of the night, being able to facilitate small groups will get easier the more you do it. Here are some helpful tips.

- Make sure that everyone is sitting in a circle together either all in chairs or all on the floor, not a mix.
- Ask good questions that cannot be answered in one word and don't be afraid of silence.
- If the youth are misbehaving address it in a loving, positive, and constructive way. If necessary remove them from the group and talk to them with the youth minister, remember to always follow your Safe Environment guidelines.
- Be a witness and an example to the youth; share your faith journey in a positive and appropriate way.

Be a witness and an example to the youth and share your faith journey.

TIMES OF PRAYER AND REFLECTION

When the Break activities include any time of prayer or reflection, it is essential that you are a good example and witness. The youth will follow your lead so be attentive to your own actions and behavior.

- Fully participate in times of group prayer such as the rosary or adoration.
- When the youth are doing reflection activities quietly pray or walk around the room. This is not a time to socialize with other Core Members.
- Positively correct any inappropriate behavior or disrespectfulness.

SEND

This portion of the Edge Night is when everything is wrapped up and the youth are ready to be sent back home. The Send activities for an Edge Night will vary greatly but there are some things that are important to keep in mind.

- Be attentive to the wrap up activities and fully participate in the closing prayer.
- Say goodbye to the youth and invite them to the next Edge Night, this is another great opportunity for relational ministry.
- Stick around and help clean up.

AFTER THE EDGE NIGHTS

FOLLOW UP

It is important to meet as a Core Team for a few minutes at the end of the Edge Night to go over how the night went. This is a good time to give suggestions, to share glory stories, or to share what was a struggle or difficult. This does not have to be an official meeting but more of a touching base so that the Core Team can improve for the next Edge Night.

RETREATS

There is usually at least one Edge retreat a year and as a Core Member you should be there for it. This is an incredible time to get to know the youth better and to really help them to get away from their everyday life and grow in their relationship with Christ. Here are a few things to keep in mind with retreats.

- Come prepared for your specific tasks and to be present to the youth.
- Be on time for all the sessions and Core Team meetings.
- Be an example for the youth and fully participate, and they will follow your lead.
- Know and follow all Safe Environment expectations and guidelines.

CONTINUE YOUR PERSONAL GROWTH

Your duties as a Core Member may seem to be done once the last youth has left the Edge Night, but your duties as a Catholic man or woman are never done. There is always somewhere to continue your spiritual and personal growth. Remember that you can only give what you have so do not forget to take time for yourself in between all your duties as a Core Member to revamp and refresh.

> Your duties as a Catholic man or woman are never done.

The most important thing you can bring, as a Core Member, to your youth group is the best you possible. This does not mean that you have to be perfect because holiness is always a continuous journey, but it does mean that you take care of your own spiritual growth. Edge Nights should not be the only time you read the Scriptures or learn about the teachings of the Catholic Church, but you should continue to pursue these things on your own. There are so many resources and books available to help you grow as a person in your faith. Remember that you are not alone; you have your Core Members, your youth minister, and the community of the Church to rely on for strength in this wonderful journey in growing closer to Christ.

Here are some helpful resources:

- Sacred Scripture (read the Daily Readings and/or Liturgy of the Hours)
- *Catechism of the Catholic Church*
- *Youcat*
- *Because God is Real* - Peter Kreeft
- *Mere Christianity* - C.S. Lewis
- *Truth be Told* - Mark Hart & Joe Cady
- *Bible Basics for Catholics* - Dr. John Bergsma
- *Hurt, 2.0* - Chap Clark
- *Blessed are the Bored in Spirit* - Mark Hart
- *Worth the Wait* - Life Teen
- *Fundamentals of the Faith* - Peter Kreeft
- *Rising Knight/Ladies First* - Natalie Tansill & Michael Specht, Life Teen
- *Finding Yourself in Scripture* - Mark Hart
- *Encounter: Experiencing God in the Everyday* - Ascension Press
- *Theology of the Body for Middle School* - Ascension Press

LIFE BEYOND EDGE NIGHTS

BY ALYSHIA KOERNER

Remember that awkward moment when you first saw your teacher out and about at a restaurant, grocery store, or the mall and you thought to yourself, "Wow, they have to eat and go shopping like 'normal' people, too?" In the world of youth ministry, we, too, find ourselves in situations in which our dear youth see us, and think, "Wow, you have a life outside of the Church building? Crazy!" These public moments allow for the youth to see us living out our Catholic faith in the secular world. However, it is not just about when the youth see us, it is about making sure our lifestyle reflects what we teach the youth. It is important to always ask yourself "Am I living out the Catholic faith in all areas of my life?"

"Wow, they have to eat and go shopping like 'normal' people, too?"

Although most middle school youth have yet to enter into the realm of social media, their "stalking" days via Facebook and Twitter are just around the corner. So it is important to take time to evaluate how you are representing yourself on social media.

- What do you say to your friends and followers on social media?
- What pictures or comments do you post?
- Are we true to who we are and what we preach at church, or are we hypocrites?

The youth will not listen to anything you have to say, or trust you for that matter, if they see you living a life that is contrary to what you are preaching at church. This goes along with the age old saying of "practice what you preach." You must be authentic in the witness of your life, you cannot ask anything of the youth that you yourself are not willing to do.

Believe it or not, our youth desire to see the Faith being lived out by those that they respect, love, and that they think are, in general...just awesome. That is right, they think you are awesome. They are looking to you as an example of how to live a Catholic life outside of church. They need to see that it is possible to be holy in the secular world and thus every aspect of your life should reflect that you are Catholic. This is no easy task but you have been given the strength of Christ by your Baptism to live out your faith. Never forget that no one is perfect, and you are not expected to be. The most important thing is that you try and commit to live the lifestyle of the Gospels. A lifestyle that radiates Christ and your Catholic faith whether you are at school, the workplace, out on the town, or at home.

Commit to live the lifestyle of the Gospels.

So how do we do this? How do we live the life we desire our youth to emulate and carry out in their day-to-day experiences? To start we cannot be afraid to live out our faith. In Scripture, the phrase, "Be not afraid," occurs over 350 times. Blessed John Paul II, during his pontificate, restated the importance of this over and over. Be not afraid.

- We have to live out our Catholic faith unashamed.
- We cannot fear what others will think of us when they see us bow our head in prayer at the office or do the sign of the cross before we eat a meal out in public.
- We cannot fear how others will respond when we share our faith with them.
- We must not be afraid to speak truth with love when others ask us questions or say something that is not true about our Catholic traditions.

In ministry, we are constantly teaching our youth to pray. We encourage them to make the time for communication with God. Again, we must practice what we preach. For those of us in school or at the office, having Christian music blasting from your computer while you work may not be tolerated. Most of you may not be able to take a break to pray the rosary, get to Mass, or complete a Holy Hour in adoration.

So the question is, how do we make time for prayer in such an environment? We spend most of our days at work or at school, so it is important that we find ways to take time to stop and pray. Here are some practical ideas to think about as a few ways to incorporate prayer into your day-to-day life:

- *Make a sticky note.* Put a simple prayer on it. Place it somewhere you will see a few times a day and take the time to pray it each time you see it.

- *Daily Readings.* Take time to dive into Scripture and read the daily Mass readings on your lunch break or when you need a brain break. You can find the readings for the day on many different Catholic websites.

- *Praise God.* If you hear others taking the Lord's name in vain, take a moment to praise God (at whatever volume you feel is appropriate for your work/school environment).

- *Traditional prayers.* Sometimes when work is overwhelming it helps to stop what you are doing, take a breath, and recite one of the traditional prayers of our Faith.

- *Pray before meals.* Whether you are out with co-workers or chillin' out in the cafeteria, take a moment to bow your head, make the sign of the cross, and thank God for your gifts and blessings.

It is really about taking the time to allow Him to enter into our day, no matter where we find ourselves.

There are many other ways to build and foster our own relationship with God throughout our days. It really is about taking the time to allow Him to enter into our day, no matter where we find ourselves, and not being ashamed to do these things in front of others. Who knows, maybe someone will ask you about what you are doing and you will have the opportunity to evangelize!

PART 4 : TAKING IT FURTHER

1. What are your strengths and where would they be best utilized during an Edge Night?

_____

_____

_____

_____

_____

2. How does relational ministry make your job easier when it comes to an Edge Night?

_____

_____

_____

_____

_____

3. What is one area where your Core Team as a whole can improve?

_____

_____

_____

_____

_____

NOW GO

THIS IS JUST THE BEGINNING

This may be the end of this book, but it is just the beginning of your journey to being the best possible you, and the best possible Core Member. This is the moment when you take a deep breath and begin to reflect on all the suggestions and tips you were just given. Some of you may have heard things like this a thousand times, and for some of you this may be the first time you are really evaluating your life and ministry in this way. No matter where you are at in your journey, the important thing is that you begin. You can read this book over and over again and think that it all sounds like a great tips, but none of this will matter unless you start applying these things to your own life.

This may be the end of this book, but it is just the beginning of your journey.

As Jesus Christ left this earth and ascended into heaven, He left His apostles with their final mission to "go, therefore, and make disciples of all nations, baptizing them in the name of the Father, and of the Son, and of the Holy Spirit, teaching them to observe all that I have commanded you" (Matthew 28:19).

By your own Baptism you have also been brought into this mission to go and tell the world the Good News, this includes the call you are currently answering to: go and tell all the crazy middle school youth the Good News. But do not worry, for by your Baptism you were also given all the graces necessary to carry out this mission, and Christ promises that He will be with us every step of the way, "Behold, I am with you always, until the end of the age" (Matthew 28:20).

"Behold, I am with you always until the end of the age" (Mt. 28:20).

So this is it. It is time to get back out there and do what you do best as a Core Member.

Always remember that you are so essential to your Edge program and that you have a specific gift to offer that no one else can. Do not be afraid; these youth need your boldness, your fearlessness, and most especially your love. Christ has called you for this specific ministry and He will give you everything you need to do it and do it well: "It was not you who chose me, but I who chose you" (John 15:15). God has a plan for you specifically and a reason that He called you to this ministry. So remember, Edge is a big commitment but it is also filled with many rewards. So be ready for all the wonderful things that God has in store for you!

These youth need your boldness, your fearlessness, and most especially your love.

BONUS MATERIALS

LEARNING TO LAUGH

Laughter truly is a gift from God, and sometimes at the end of a less than glamorous Edge Night it is all we are able to do. Working with middle school youth is one of the greatest challenges but also one of the greatest gold mines for funny stories! So if you are finding yourself at your wit's end and everything you have tried has failed, just learn to laugh, because after it all you will probably have a great story to tell. Here are just a few examples of such stories.

MIDDLE SCHOOL MATH: CANDY + YOUTH = TROUBLE

BY BRADLEY OPITZ

To most youth ministers, I would be considered a veteran to the game. I have been a youth minister for almost seven years, working with both high school and middle school students at different parishes around the country. I have been involved with many aspects of middle school ministry and I would like to consider myself knowledgeable in the ways of the do's and don'ts when it comes to putting on Edge Nights. But sometimes, with all my knowledge of youth ministry, I have a lapse in judgment. This is a story of such a lapse.

Last fall, just a few weeks after Halloween, a fellow catechist at the parish was given a box full of candy and was not sure what to do with it. She did not want to keep it in her office because she knew if she did, she would end up eating most of the box. She came by my office, as she does about once a week and asked a very worn and sometimes over used question, "Hey, do you want this? I have no need for it." I took the box and sorted through the contents for a second and being a resourceful person I thought to myself, "Yeah, I could use this for Edge tonight." If you have been around middle school youth long enough, you would know that giving them large amounts of candy during an Edge Night should be done with utmost caution. Therefore in all my knowledge and wisdom I took the box and hid it in the youth room until I needed it later in the night.

He grabbed it with both hands, held it over his head, and yelled, "I found CANDY!!!!"

The evening rolled around and the youth began to trickle in. As they waited for Edge to begin, some students played Ping-Pong, others air hockey, and pockets of girls talked in groups around the room. Then there was that one kid, and you all know the one I am talking about. In just about every youth group there is at least one or two of these youth that manage to always get into things that they have no business getting into. Just as the night was about to get underway this particular boy found the box of candy where it had been so masterfully hidden. He grabbed it with both hands, held it over his head, and yelled, "I found CANDY!!!!" Like a dog whistle it caught the attention of every kid in that room. I should have known better, and what was soon to follow was a rookie mistake.

So how could I, in all my wisdom and knowledge, have ever let this happen, you may ask. Well I had been having trouble getting the attention of a few of the middle school youth during talks and small group discussions. My thought was that I could take the candy and instill positive reinforcement among them by giving candy to the youth who participated. Every time a student answered a question correctly, they would receive a piece of candy. According to adolescent psychologists, it is typically good to reward positive behavior. But what is not included in this psychological study was the negative effect of that much sugar on middle school youth. Even though most of the youth had already had their fair share of candy, I continued to give them pieces of candy during my talk as they answered questions correctly. As the candy was flowing, they slowly became more and more crazy and out of control. By the end of the teaching not one middle school student could sit still and a few of them began to raid the box again as if they were reenacting the 1992 Los Angeles riots.

The Edge Night slowly began to turn into a scene from the "Lord Of The Flies."

All that could be done in that moment was to watch in horror as the Edge Night slowly began to turn into a scene from the "Lord Of The Flies." As the chaos ensued we quickly drew a plan because we knew the whole night was about to be lost, and the candy had to be moved out of the room. In order to pull this off, I played upon one of the token qualities of middle school youth, their short attention spans. As we broke for small groups I nonchalantly grabbed the box of candy and gave it to my most responsible high school student who smuggled it out of the room. Thankfully this actually worked and most of the youth did not even notice it was gone – probably due to slight sugar comas.

During small groups some of the middle school youth began to calm down while others were still feeling the effects of the sugar rushing through their veins. At this point, the small groups were not very effective. As the night started to come to an end and parents started lining up outside of the room to pick up their student, I was glad to know that this night was almost over. Once the last kid was picked up and we met as a Core Team for a post-Edge meeting, we were all exhausted. During the meeting we all came to the conclusion, as we ate the rest of the candy, that never again would we use candy to get the youth to talk.

SPOILED MILK AND CHERRIES

BY MANDA POFFEL

Whipped cream smells like spoiled milk and maraschino cherries stain your skin. These are a few things I have learned the hard way.

I was looking for a new prize for games during the Gather of my Edge Night, and I realized that sugaring up my youth then going right into the Proclaim wasn't working so well. There were countless days when we would sit together as a Core Team and ask the tough question, "How can we capture the joy of Edge more? What can we do to engage them more?" And the answer we came up with was simple: pie.

It made me smile thinking of the countless people I had seen get pied in the face or turned into human sundaes.

I remembered when we pied some Core Members at Life Teen and how it went over amazingly well, so I decided this would go over **really** well with middle school youth. It made me smile thinking of the countless people I had seen get pied in the face or turned into human sundaes. And I remembered thinking how funny it is when such things happen, as long as it is to someone else.

So it came to that night at Edge, and these fateful words simply fell from my mouth during the Gather that night: "Oh, the winning small group of this relay race gets to pie Manda and a Core Member of their choice in the face next week!" That's the moment I remembered that my name is Manda, and I just threw myself under the bus. I hadn't intended for this to happen, but alas I was going to be the one I always laughed at.

The next week, when the winning small group came forward, I realized that my assistant, who had just finished dressing me in a trash bag with a hole cut in the top, had little surprises for me. Those surprises were maraschino cherries and graham cracker crusts contained inside my whipped creamed fate. I stepped onto the stage and took a deep breath as the girls stepped forward and pressed the disgusting mixture into my face. I also felt that—oh so refreshing—feeling of fingers combing through my hip length hair-with whipped cream. Insert gagging noise here as the aroma of spoiled milk began to surround me.

After I managed to open my eyes in the midst of the gunk and cherries, I saw that the middle schoolers had that crazy look in their eyes and asked them, "Are you satisfied now?" That was the wrong question to ask. The overwhelming response screamed at me down below was, "NOOOO!" So, I did what any evangelist with an ounce of self-depreciating humor would do: I put on a huge smile and chased a couple of the small group members off stage threatening them with a hug. There was cheering and laughter and they were satisfied. I introduced the speaker for the night and made my way into our kitchen where I used the faucet more like a hose.

It is important that we are never afraid of failure.

After the night was over and I had gone home to at least two showers, which still didn't do the trick, I recognized the beauty in such a crazy act. Over my years with middle school youth, I've learned a lot of things. One of those things is that putting myself in a position to be human, which is vital to ministry. Humanity is something we need to remember to show our youth all the time. It is important that we are never so afraid of failure, or the smell of spoiled milk, that we forget to step out and take a chance with middle school youth. It is important that we are all humble enough to show that we are human and willing to be crazy and silly and messy.

TRUST ME, FALL ON

BY NATALIE TANSILL

The first time I looked around a packed room of middle school youth, I mistakenly felt a little over confident. I thought to myself this is going to be easy. I was taller than three quarters of the room, and I thought I could relate to them by talking about things I remembered from middle school... like N'SYNC and other outdated pop stars. I was cool when I was in middle school, so I thought it couldn't be that hard.

It was my first week as a Summer Missionary at Covecrest. We had just finished our week of formation, prayed to prepare ourselves for all the souls that were coming to camp, and I thought I had it all figured out.

But, oh the Lord likes to keep me humble.

I walked up to the group of girls I was assigned to for the week and the closer I got to them, the more intensely I could feel their stares of death. My confidence was slowly escaping me when I quickly realized that no one in the group would speak to each other. Oh gosh, I hated drama and here I was stepping into a mess of passive aggressive silence.

I was cool when I was in middle school, so I thought it couldn't be that hard.

Praise God I had another summer missionary, Nicole, to help maneuver the hormonal group. Trying to get them to answer questions during small group was like pulling teeth. Not only would they not participate in conversation... but we had to lead them on a low ropes obstacle course.

You might be wondering what low ropes are.... Well they are community building activities that REQUIRE groups to act like a team to reach a common goal.

It was a cloudy and rainy day and the girls were talking about how "they didn't feel like participating." Nicole (who is now Sister Peter

Thomas!) and I were doing everything we could to stay cheerful... but had now clue how to get these girls to participate.

Then we walked up to the trust fall, which consists of a three-foot platform that one person stands and falls backwards into the arms of their group that catches them, hence learning to trust them. This is usually everyone's favorite activity, but none of the girls were willing to do it. "You'll drop me." "I don't want to." "I don't want to stand next to her." You name it, they whined about it.

She hit our hands, but then something went wrong.

Out of sheer desperation, my fellow summer missionary and I finally convinced them that anyone could do it... even one of us. Nicole got up on the three-foot high platform explaining how easy it would be in hopes that they would follow her lead.

"I trust you," Nicole proclaimed from the platform with her back towards us on the ground.

"Trust us, fall on" we yelled back... and by "we," it was more like me.

Hands crossed and feet together Nicole began her fall.

She hit our hands, but then something went wrong.

She kept falling, until she hit the ground. It's a good thing that those of us catching her were all about five feet tall so her fall wasn't too far.

Her body hit the floor.

She sat up and began to laugh. Her fall broke the tension and all we could do was laugh with her. Our plan may not have worked the way that we thought it would... but for some reason the girls wanted to try it again to prove that they could do it.

Then conversations just started flowing. "I have anger problems and I just need to trust that God is bigger than my problems." "I was so mad that my mom made me come, but I trust that God wants me here now." "I have issues trusting that God loves me."

What?!

Here we were trying to do everything we could think of to convince them to see God, when all we had to do was just be authentic. That trust fall started a flow of honest conversations and they shared how God was working in them that week.

I'd like to say that I saw it coming... but that'd be a lie.

You can't persuade someone into falling in love with God. All you can do is witness to it and share how great His love and mercy is. I thought I had to impress them with my humor, but all I had to do was just be me. At the end of the week, I remember sitting and reflecting on how that trust fall was not just for them, but for me as well. God wanted to remind me to trust Him — trust that no matter how difficult the outreach might be at times, it's all about falling more in love with Him. That's what makes ministry work, on that foundation.

I just had to trust God even when my plan failed; He had a bigger plan in motion.

No matter how difficult the outreach might be at times, it's all about falling more in love with Him.

In ministry, it can be easy to get discouraged by difficult teens or situations. But never forget that when we say, "Jesus, I trust You" His response is always, "Trust Me, fall on."

CAPRI SUNS AND PUPPIES
BY ALISON GRISWOLD

After Msgr. Gregory of Mustard Seed Communities spoke at all our Masses one weekend, I asked the middle schoolers what they thought about his mission helping children in developing countries. My hope was that they would want to help. The conversation went something like this:

"Miss Alison! You know how you can buy a star? We could BUY a poor KID!"

"So, who heard Msgr. Gregory at Mass this weekend?"

I was greeted by a chorus of, "I didn't go to Mass this weekend."

(Insert tangent of, "I know you're in sixth grade, but you need to remind your parents how important it is to take you to Mass on Sunday or Saturday night if your soccer coaches are heathens who don't observe the Sabbath. I'm sure you have a similar script in your pocket.)

"Well, if you didn't hear Msgr. Gregory for yourself, he talked about the children that his mission takes care of in Jamaica, The Dominican Republic, Nicaragua and Zimbabwe who don't have enough to eat. There's a program where we can support them called Sustain a Life. Wouldn't that be a nice thing for us to do?"

Mikey, a sixth grader, excitedly raises his hand and waves it frantically around. He's such a compassionate child; I knew he'd be the first to want to help. Not even waiting for me to call on him, Mikey blurts out, "Miss Alison! You know how you can buy a star? We could BUY a poor KID!"

This idea is met with great excitement. Nicole, a seventh grader, chimes in, "Yeah! We could keep it here in the youth room. They could sleep on the couch and you could be its MOM!"

This is not going in the direction I had hoped, but thinking it was still salvageable, I tried to bring them back to the reality of the situation, asking, "well, that's really nice of you guys to want to take care of a kid, but don't you think they'd miss their family, living in the youth room?"

The kids stare at me, blankly. "No," they all say. "They could play the Wii."

I persist, although I can feel my teeth starting to grind. These children WILL learn the richness of Catholic Social Teaching and the principle of subsidiarity. So I ask, "You wouldn't want to leave your family and live in the youth room, would you? Even if you had cool stuff, wouldn't you miss them?"

Again, a blank stare and a chorus of, "no."

Still, I am prepared with a plan of action. A way for them to put their faith into motion and sacrifice for others that I am convinced will stir their hearts to serve the common good. "Well, guys, we can't keep a kid here" (this is met with a round of disappointed sighs) "but we can send them money each month to help feed the kids in Zimbabwe! Isn't that cool? What about if, for the next month, instead of drinking Capri Suns, we drink water and sent the money to feed a child in Zimbabwe?"

"You mean bottled water?" they ask.

"No, that still costs money. I'd give you a cup and you could get water from the water fountain," I explain.

This is met with looks of incredulity and a round of, "No, I don't think so...." At this point, I'm rapidly losing faith in humanity and, specifically, the 6th grade. Hands on my hips, I sternly ask, "You guys, when you die and Jesus asks you how you took care of each other, don't you want to say that you gave up Capri Suns so that kids in Zimbabwe could eat?"

"Well, maybe if we could have hot chocolate instead?" Nicole suggests.

Then, Mikey remembers something. "Miss Alison! You can sponsor a puppy for $15 a month! And they send you a hoodie and a tote bag! That's even cheaper! Could we keep a puppy in the youth room?"

I sigh. "You know what guys, let's just put in a movie."

As exasperating as this was, it is exactly what I love about middle school students. Their minds and hearts are so open and conversations range from inspiring to completely absurd. We can't run from this critical moment in Catholic formation—when ideas are being tested and virtue formed—just because it's a little chaotic and full of dizzying logic. Investing in the lives of middle schoolers is essential. When we meet students here, forming relationships over puppy dogs and Capri Suns, we help establish a relationship with the Church that they can lean into as they mature into Catholic adults.

Their minds and hearts are so open and conversations range from inspiring to completely absurd.